ESSENTIAL DK COMPUTERS

SPREADSHEETS

CHARTS & GRAPHICS

ABOUT THIS BOOK

Charts and Graphics is for people who already have a basic understanding of Microsoft's Excel 2000 spreadsheet program, including opening a new worksheet, entering data, and saving.

As well as being a powerful spreadsheet program, Microsoft® Excel 2000 offers a wide range of facilities that allow you to show numerical data in the form of two-and three-dimensional charts. Through the Excel Drawing toolbar, you can also create graphics combining shapes, color, and decorative text to bring your worksheets and charts to life. This book is a concise guide to these aspects of Excel, and it assumes that you have a basic knowledge of the way Excel works.

The opening chapter is a quick overview of the program, and of the Excel window and toolbars. Subsequent chapters take you through creating a chart from data, giving it a title and labelling it, moving, resizing, and updating the chart. The various possible kinds of chart (line chart, area chart, bar chart, pie chart, and many subtypes), together with the uses to which they are best suited, are then explained. Further chapters deal with formatting a chart and using the graphics tools.

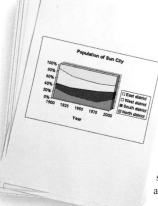

Presenting data from Excel worksheets in a visual form adds clarity and color.

Throughout the book, information is presented using step-by-step sequences. Virtually every step is accompanied by an illustration showing how your screen should look at each stage.

Some basic examples run through the book, and it may be difficult to keep track of these if you skip any sections.

Command keys, such as ENTER and CTRL, are shown in these rectangles: Enter ⏎ and Ctrl, to avoid confusion, for example, over whether you should press that key, or type the letters "ctrl." Cross-references are shown in the text as left- and right-hand page icons: ◁ and ▷. The page number and the title of the paragraph to which you are referred are shown at the foot of the page.

As well as the step-by-step sections, there are boxes that explain particular features in detail, and tip boxes that provide alternative methods and shortcuts. Finally, at the back of the book, you will find a glossary explaining new terms, and a comprehensive index.

ESSENTIAL **DK** COMPUTERS

SPREADSHEETS

CHARTS & GRAPHICS

ROBERT DINWIDDIE

A Dorling Kindersley Book

Dorling Kindersley
LONDON, NEW YORK, SYDNEY, DELHI, PARIS, MUNICH, and JOHANNESBURG

Produced for Dorling Kindersley Limited by
Design Revolution, Queens Park Villa,
30 West Drive, Brighton, East Sussex BN2 2GE

EDITORIAL DIRECTOR Ian Whitelaw
SENIOR DESIGNER Andy Ashdown
PROJECT EDITOR John Watson
DESIGNER Paul Bowler

MANAGING ART EDITOR Nigel Duffield
SENIOR EDITOR Mary Lindsay
DTP DESIGNER Jason Little
PRODUCTION CONTROLLER Wendy Penn

Published in the United States by Dorling Kindersley Publishing, Inc.
95 Madison Avenue, New York, New York, 10016

First American Edition, 2000

2 4 6 8 10 9 7 5 3 1

Published in Great Britain by Dorling Kindersley.

A catalog record is available from the Library of Congress.

ISBN 0-7894-6371-7

Color reproduced by First Impressions, London
Printed in Italy by Graphicom

For our complete
catalog visit
www.dk.com

Contents

MICROSOFT EXCEL

Excel belongs to the group of computer applications known as spreadsheets, and the first spreadsheet program started the process of making computers an indispensable business tool.

WHAT CAN EXCEL DO?

Storing spreadsheet data is only the beginning as far as Excel is concerned. The wide range of features it contains lets you manipulate and present your data in almost any way you choose. Excel can be an accounts program; it can be used as a sophisticated calculator capable of utilizing complex mathematical formulas; it can also be a diary, a scheduler, and more. Used in combination with

Microsoft Word, Excel's database features make creating mailing lists and personalized letters very easy. Excel's presentation facilities use color, borders, and different fonts to emphasize data. A variety of charts is available, which can be selected to suit the kind of data being presented. For storing, manipulating, and presenting data, Microsoft Excel offers an unrivaled range of possibilities.

WHAT IS A WORKSHEET?

At the heart of Excel is a two-dimensional grid of data storage spaces called a worksheet (right). This is where you input the data that you want to store, manipulate, or analyze. The individual spaces are called worksheet cells. To begin with, all the cells are empty. As you put data into the cells, you build and develop the individual worksheets.

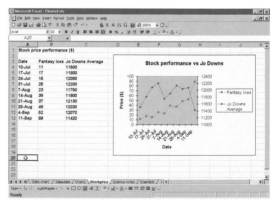

LAUNCHING EXCEL

Approaching a new program for the first time can be a daunting experience because you don't know what to expect. However, new programs are learned one step at a time and the first step is the simple one of launching Excel from your desktop.

1 LAUNCHING WITH THE START MENU

● If you are running Windows 95 or 98, click on the **Start** button at bottom left, and then choose **Programs** from the pop-up list. Microsoft Excel should appear in the submenu to the right (or it may be within a Microsoft Office Program group). Highlight the words **Microsoft Excel** and click with the mouse.

● The Excel window appears on screen .

2 LAUNCHING WITH A SHORTCUT

● If there is already a shortcut to Excel on your Desktop, just double-click on the shortcut icon.

● The Excel window appears on screen .

The Excel Window

8

THE EXCEL WINDOW

Soon after you launch Microsoft Excel, a window called **Microsoft Excel – Book1** appears. At the center of the window is a worksheet – a grid of blank rectangular cells. Letters and numbers label the columns and rows of the grid. Each cell has an address (such as E3), which is the column and row in which it is found.

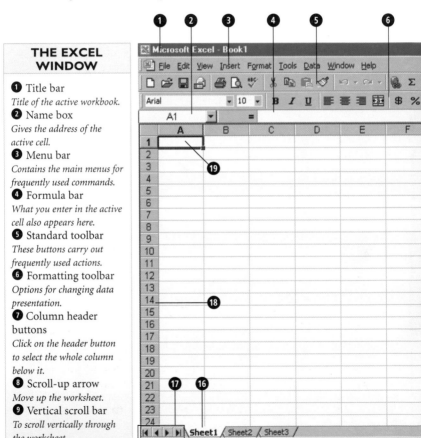

THE EXCEL WINDOW

1 Title bar
Title of the active workbook.

2 Name box
Gives the address of the active cell.

3 Menu bar
Contains the main menus for frequently used commands.

4 Formula bar
What you enter in the active cell also appears here.

5 Standard toolbar
These buttons carry out frequently used actions.

6 Formatting toolbar
Options for changing data presentation.

7 Column header buttons
Click on the header button to select the whole column below it.

8 Scroll-up arrow
Move up the worksheet.

9 Vertical scroll bar
To scroll vertically through the worksheet.

TOOLBAR LAYOUT

If Excel doesn't show the Formatting toolbar below the Standard toolbar, first place the cursor over the Formatting toolbar "handle." When the four-headed arrow appears, (right) hold down the mouse button and "drag" the toolbar into position.

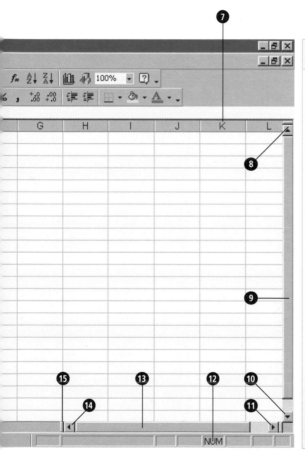

THE EXCEL WINDOW

10 Scroll-down arrow
Move down the worksheet.

11 Right-scroll arrow
Scrolls the sheet to the right.

12 NUM lock
Shows the numeric keypad on the keyboard is on.

13 Horizontal scroll bar
To scroll horizontally through the worksheet.

14 Left-scroll arrow
Scrolls the sheet to the left.

15 Tab split box
Click and drag to show tabs or to increase the scroll bar.

16 Worksheet tabs
Workbooks contain worksheets – click to select one.

17 Tab scrolling buttons
Scroll through the sheets if they cannot all be displayed.

18 Row header buttons
Click on the row header to select the entire row.

19 Active cell
Whatever you type appears in the active cell.

THE TWO MAIN EXCEL TOOLBARS

Many of the actions, or commands, that you want to perform on data can be carried out by clicking on toolbar buttons. When you launch Excel, the Standard toolbar and the Formatting toolbar are the usual toolbars displayed. They contain buttons whose actions are described below. The Standard toolbar contains buttons for actions as diverse as opening a new workbook or undoing an action. The Formatting toolbar contains buttons for changing the worksheet's appearance.

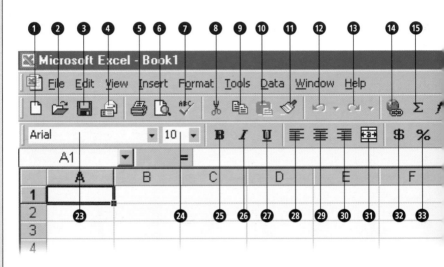

BUTTON FUNCTIONS

- ❶ New workbook
- ❷ Open file
- ❸ Save workbook
- ❹ Email workbook/sheet
- ❺ Print
- ❻ Print preview
- ❼ Spelling checker
- ❽ Cut
- ❾ Copy
- ❿ Paste
- ⓫ Format painter
- ⓬ Undo action(s)
- ⓭ Redo action(s)
- ⓮ Insert hyperlink
- ⓯ AutoSum
- ⓰ Paste function
- ⓱ Sort ascending
- ⓲ Sort descending
- ⓳ Chart wizard
- ⓴ Drawing toolbar
- ㉑ Zoom view
- ㉒ Help
- ㉓ Font selector
- ㉔ Font size selector

14 Creating a Simple Chart

56 Creating and Formatting Shapes

CUSTOMIZING A TOOLBAR

Click the arrow at far right of the Formatting toolbar, then on the arrow on the **Add or Remove Buttons** box that appears. A drop-down menu opens from which you can add or remove toolbar buttons.

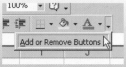

ScreenTips

It is not necessary to memorize all these buttons. Roll the cursor over a button, wait for a second, and a ScreenTip appears telling you the function of the button.

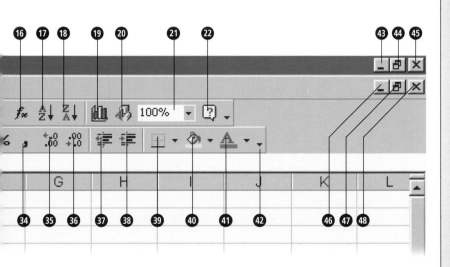

BUTTON FUNCTIONS

㉕ Bold	㉝ Percent style	㊶ Font color
㉖ Italic	㉞ Comma style	㊷ Add/remove buttons
㉗ Underline	㉟ Increase decimals	㊸ Minimize Excel
㉘ Align left	㊱ Decrease decimals	㊹ Restore Excel
㉙ Center	㊲ Decrease indent	㊺ Close Excel
㉚ Align right	㊳ Increase indent	㊻ Minimize worksheet
㉛ Merge and center	㊴ Add/remove borders	㊼ Restore worksheet
㉜ Currency style	㊵ Fill color	㊽ Close worksheet

CHART BASICS

One of the most popular and useful of Excel's features is the ability to create charts based on worksheet data. A chart, or graph, is a visual representation of selected data in a worksheet.

PARTS OF A CHART

Every Excel chart has some standard parts. Each part can be formatted separately. For example, the fonts and type sizes used for the titles can be altered, as can the background colors, the thickness of the gridlines, and so on. Some chart components can be moved around and resized relative to the other parts.

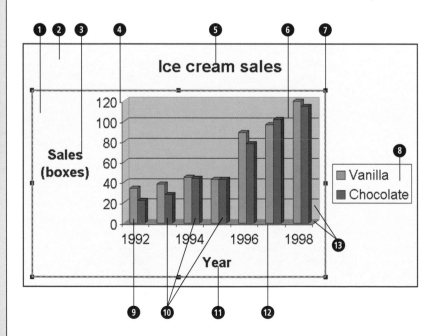

THE NAMING OF PARTS

❶ Plot Area

The plot area is a rectangular region that includes the charted data. In 3D charts, the plot area may also enclose the chart axes and the axis titles.

❷ Chart Area

The chart area includes the plot area and the surrounding space that holds the chart title and legend. When a chart is moved or resized, this involves the whole chart area.

❸ Value Axis Title

This indicates the units of measurement of the data.

❹ Value Axis ⌐|

The value axis is a line along which units of measurement used for the data are arranged. The magnitude of each piece of data (its value) is plotted against this axis. In column charts, the value axis is always the vertical axis (often called the Y axis).

❺ Chart Title

The chart title is an optional summary of the subject matter of the chart.

❻ Gridlines

The gridlines are horizontal guidelines that appear behind the plotted data and make it easier to read.

❼ Handles 📄

Handles are small black boxes that appear around the perimeter of an object after it has been selected (clicked on). The black boxes indicate that you can move, resize, format, or remove the object.

❽ Legend

The legend is a key that explains the data series in a chart.

❾ Data Marker

A data marker is a piece of data plotted on a chart. It corresponds to the information in a single worksheet cell. A data marker may be a single column, a small cross or square, or a pie "slice," depending on the type of chart.

❿ Data Series

A data series is a collection of data markers. It usually corresponds to the data within a column or row of cells in a worksheet. A data series might

be seen on a chart as a series of columns, or as a series of small squares or crosses joined by a line. In this chart there are two data series – sales of vanilla ice cream, and sales of chocolate ice cream.

⓫ Category Axis Title

This indicates the nature of the chart's categories.

⓬ Category Axis ⌐|

The category axis is a line along which labels for the chart's categories are arranged. In broad terms, categories are individual measurement intervals or groupings for the original charted data. For this chart, the categories are the years 1992–1998. In column charts, the category axis is the horizontal line (X axis) along the bottom of the chart.

⓭ Walls and Floor

In 3D charts, the boundaries of the region defined by the chart's axes are called the walls and floor. They can be formatted separately from the remainder of the plot area.

SCREEN RESOLUTION

It is best to use a high screen resolution (1024 x 768 pixels or above) for creating charts in Excel and for the exercises in this book. To check screen resolution, click with the right mouse button on a blank area of your Desktop and choose **Properties** in the pop-up menu. In the **Display Properties** dialog box, choose the **Settings** tab and then inspect the **Screen area** section.

| 46 | **Formatting the Axes** | | 21 | **Moving the chart** |

CREATING A SIMPLE CHART

Creating a chart in Excel is a very straight-forward procedure. To do this, you need to use a subprogram called the Chart Wizard, which will guide you through every stage in the process. The Chart Wizard consists of a series of dialog boxes, which prompt you to make decisions such as what type of chart to use, what axes you want to use for the chart, how you would like to label the chart axes, and where you would like to display the chart. In this section, you will use the Chart Wizard to create a simple column chart. To begin, open a new Excel workbook and save it under the name **Charts.xls**. Rename Sheet1 in the workbook **Salesdata**.

1 SELECTING DATA FOR A CHART

● To create any chart, you first need some kind of data. For this example, enter the data on vanilla and chocolate ice cream sales (shown at right) into the **Salesdata** worksheet of your **Charts.xls** workbook. If you want to give the entered data more emphasis, you can select it all and click the **Bold** button on the Standard toolbar, as we have done in this example.

Microsoft Excel - Charts

File Edit View Insert Format Tools Data Window Help

Arial · 10 · **B** *I* U ≡ ≡ ≡ ≡ %

M31 =

	A	B	C	D	E
1	Ice Cream Sales (boxes)				
2					
3		Vanilla	Chocolate		
4	1992	34	22		
5	1993	38	28		
6	1994	45	44		
7	1995	43	43		
8	1996	89	78		
9	1997	97	102		
10	1998	120	115		
11	1999	106	139		
12					

CHARTABLE DATA

Excel can create chart data series only from values that it recognizes as numerical values.

Ordinary numbers (such as 45, 0.32, or 1765) are always recognized as numerical values, but be aware that numbers accompanied by units (for example 52 secs or 24 cents) are usually not.

● Now select just the data you want to chart, including relevant row and column labels (but not any overall worksheet title). In this case, let's suppose you want to chart the sales data from 1992–1998. To do this, select cells A3 to C10 (click cell A3, hold down the ⇧ Shift key, and then click cell C10).

	A	B	C	D	E
1	Ice Cream Sales (boxes)				
2					
3		Vanilla	Chocolate		
4	1992	34	22		
5	1993	38	28		
6	1994	45	44		
7	1995	43	43		
8	1996	89	78		
9	1997	97	102		
10	1998	120	115		
11	1999	106	139		
12					

2 CHOOSE CHART WIZARD BUTTON

● The next step is very simple – just click the **Chart Wizard** button on the Standard toolbar. It is a brightly colored button featuring what appears to be a small chart, consisting of tiny blue, yellow, and red columns ⌐.

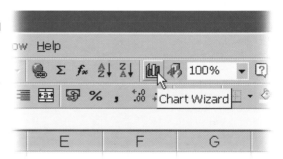

3 CHOOSE THE CHART TYPE

● The first Chart Wizard dialog box appears. In the section at left, under **Chart type:**, is a list of the main types of charts available. Click in turn on a number of these to see the range of options available.

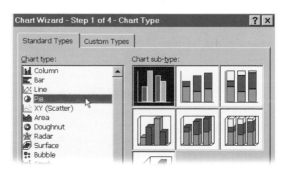

⑲ Chart Wizard

● Finish by clicking on the word **Column** at the top of the list to confirm that you want a Column chart.

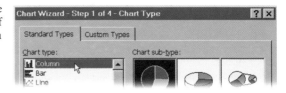

4 CHOOSE THE CHART SUB-TYPE

● Now choose between the available sub-types of Column chart. On this occasion, click on the middle option in the left-hand column, which is described in a box below as a **Clustered column with a 3-D visual effect**.

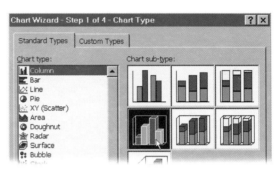

5 PREVIEW YOUR CHOSEN CHART

● For a preview of how your data will look as a chart, click on the button labeled **Press and Hold to View Sample**, holding down the mouse button as you do so. Then release the mouse button and click on **Next** to pass to the next dialog box.

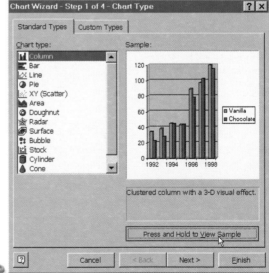

6 CONFIRM THE SOURCE DATA

The next dialog box contains another chart preview, and a box labeled **Data range**, in which **Salesdata!$A$3:$C$10** appears. This means that the source data for your chart is contained in the block of cells from A3 to C10 in the **Salesdata** worksheet.

● To the right of the words **Series in** are two option buttons, **Rows** and **Columns**. These refer to two different choices for presenting your chart. At present, **Columns** is checked. To see an alternative presentation, click the **Rows** option.

● This option groups the sales data for the two ice cream products separately instead of comparing them directly year-by-year. To return to the previous view, click back on **Columns**, and then on **Next**.

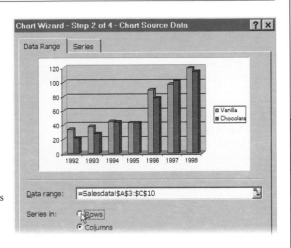

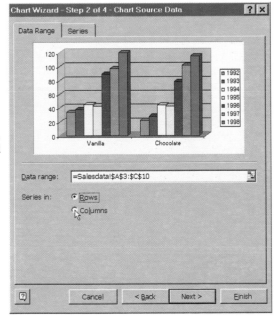

7 CHOOSE A TITLE AND AXIS LABELS

The next dialog box prompts you to give your chart a title and name its axes.

● Click in the **Chart title** box and type **Ice cream sales**.

● Click in the **Category (X) axis** box. Here you should type a descriptive label for the bottom (X) axis of your chart. In this case type **Year**.

● Finally, click in the **Value (Z) axis** box. For this chart, the vertical axis is the Z axis. Type **Sales (boxes)**. Then click on **Next**.

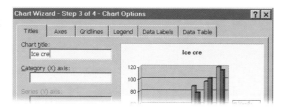

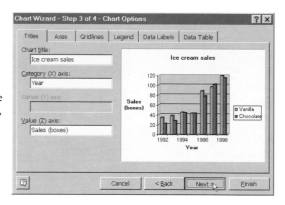

8 CHOOSE CHART LOCATION

The final dialog box asks whether you would like your chart **As new sheet**, which means it will occupy a sheet of its own, or **As object in: Salesdata**, which means you can place it in an area of the Salesdata worksheet, right next to its source data. For this example, you would like your chart as an object, so just click on **Finish**.

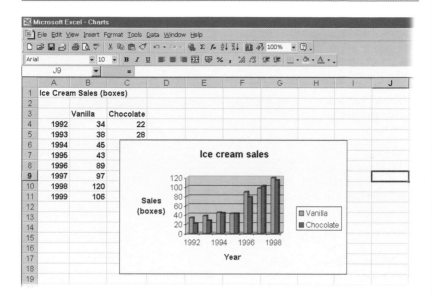

● You should now see the chart in the **Salesdata** worksheet, as this screen shot shows. Click the **Save** button on the Standard toolbar ⬚. (The chart may be obscuring some of the data on the source worksheet, but in the next section ⬚ we will see how to move the chart or change its size to solve this.)

MYSTERIOUS DOLLAR SIGNS

You will sometimes come across references to cells or cell ranges in Excel that contain puzzling dollar signs – for example $A$15. References containing these signs are called absolute cell references and they indicate that the reference is always to the indicated cell, no matter where the source of the reference might be moved around in the worksheet. So, $A$15 simply means "the value in cell A15."

There is another type of cell reference, called a relative cell reference, that contains no dollar signs and indicates a cell's position *relative* to the cell from where the reference is being made. For example the reference "C8" in cell A8 actually means "the value in the cell two cells to the right of this one." Relative cell references are extremely useful for worksheets containing a lot of formulas, but generally you don't need to worry about them for charting purposes.

10 ❸ **Save workbook**

20 **Moving and Resizing an Embedded Chart**

MOVING AND RESIZING AN EMBEDDED CHART

After you have placed a chart as an object in a worksheet (such as the chart you created on pages 14–19) you can move it to a convenient location and also resize it in various ways. Try these techniques on your ice cream sales chart.

1 SELECT WHOLE CHART AREA

● Click in a blank area near any corner of the chart area .

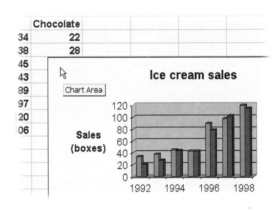

● You will see handles (small black squares) appear within the perimeter of the chart area. These indicate that the chart area has been selected. You will also see some colored borders appear around the worksheet data that you have turned into a chart.

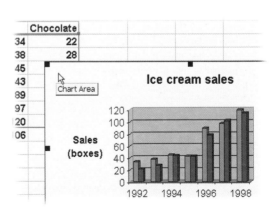

❷ **Chart area**   ❼ **Handles**

2 MOVING THE CHART

● Click and hold down the mouse button in a blank area toward a corner of the chart area. The mouse pointer should turn into four arrows in a compass arrangement.

● Still holding down the mouse button, drag the mouse in the direction that you wish to move the chart. You should see an outline of the chart move with the mouse pointer.

● Once the outline is in the desired location, release the mouse button to "drop" the chart at that location.

● You might now like to enlarge the chart by dragging a corner handle.

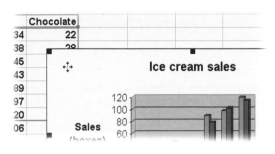

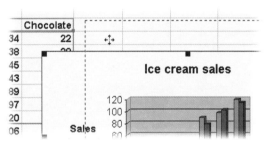

SIDE AND CORNER HANDLES

To resize a chart in one dimension only (for example, width or depth), drag a handle situated along one of the sides of the selected chart area. To resize your chart in two dimensions (both width and depth), drag a handle at a corner of the selected chart area.

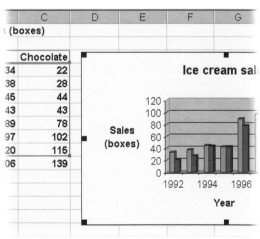

CHART OPTIONS

There are many different ways of presenting and modifying a chart, and a simple way to choose between some standard options is by using the **Chart Options** command and dialog box. Try performing the following modifications.

1 ACCESSING CHART OPTIONS

● Click in a blank area near any corner of the chart area to select the whole chart area .
● Choose **Chart Options** from the Chart menu.
● The **Chart Options** dialog box appears.

VARIOUS CHART OPTIONS

Different sections of the **Chart Options** dialog box allow you to add additional gridlines or vertical gridlines , add labels to data markers, or add a data table (like a mini-spreadsheet) to your chart. For more extensive modifications to the way your chart looks (for example the color scheme), you should select the part to modify and then use the **Selected...** command from the **Format** menu.

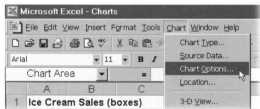

2 CHANGING AN AXIS TITLE

● To change the title of an axis, click immediately after the word **Year** in the entry field under **Category (X) axis:**. Type a space and then type in (**to October 31**).

● Within a second or two, you will see the miniature version of the chart within the dialog box update to show the new axis title 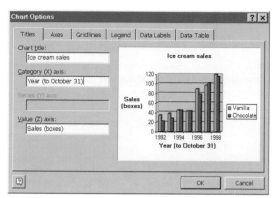.

3 MOVING THE LEGEND

● Click the **Legend** tab at the top of the dialog box.

● In the **Legend** section, click on the **Top** option button.

● You will immediately see the legend move from the right of the chart to above the chart.

● Now click on **OK** to confirm your changes.

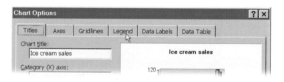

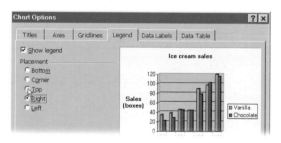

Experiment…

The **Chart Options** dialog box is a good place to experiment with the presentation of your chart. If your ideas don't work out, you can always just click on **Cancel** and try again.

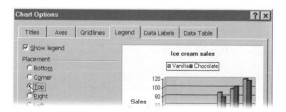

⓫ **Category Axis Title**

UPDATING THE SOURCE DATA

One of Excel's great strengths as a charting tool is that you can update the chart's worksheet source data and see the change reflected immediately in the chart. This can be done without having to reactivate the **Chart Wizard**. You can also extend the range of cells within your source data that are charted, and again see the chart update immediately. Follow these steps to see how these modifications work.

1 CHANGING A PIECE OF DATA

● Click on cell B6 in your worksheet to select this cell. It currently contains the value 45 representing sales of boxes of vanilla ice cream in 1994.

Click on cell B6

	A	B	C	D	E
1	Ice Cream Sales (boxes)				
2					
3		Vanilla	Chocolate		
4	1992	34	22		
5	1993	38	28		
6	1994	45	44		
7	1995	43	43		

● We are going to suppose that sales of 20 extra boxes were overlooked when the original figure was keyed in. Type **65** to correct this mistake, and then press $\boxed{\text{Enter} \leftarrow}$ while looking at your chart to see the effect of changing the value.

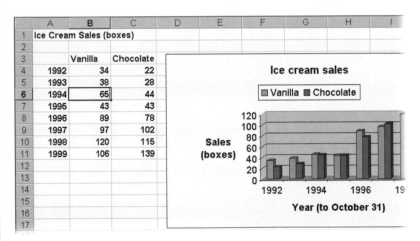

● The blue column in the chart representing vanilla ice cream sales in 1994 immediately shoots up.

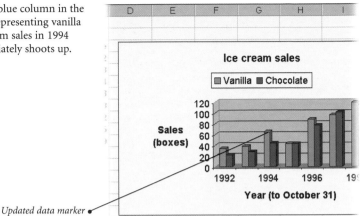

Updated data marker ●

2 EXTENDING THE DATA RANGE

● Click toward a corner of the chart area to select it. Colored borders will appear around the range of your worksheet data that has been charted. At present only the sales from 1992 to 1998 have been charted.

	A	B	C	D	E
1	Ice Cream Sales (boxes)				
2					
3		Vanilla	Chocolate		
4	1992	34	22		
5	1993	38	28		Chart Area
6	1994	65	44		
7	1995	43	43		

● Place your mouse pointer at the corner of the data range that you wish to extend – in this case at the bottom right of cell C10. You should see the pointer turn into a small plus sign.

	A	B	C	D	E
1	Ice Cream Sales (boxes)				
2					
3		Vanilla	Chocolate		
4	1992	34	22		
5	1993	38	28		
6	1994	65	44		
7	1995	43	43		
8	1996	89	78		
9	1997	97	102		
10	1998	120	115		Sales
11	1999	106	139		(boxes)
12					

Pointer turns into plus sign ●

● Press down on the mouse button and drag the mouse down until the colored borders extend to encompass cells in row 11.

● Release the mouse button and you should see your chart update to include the 1999 data.

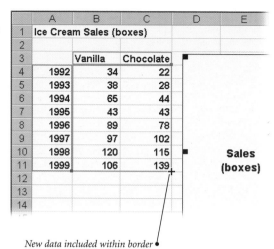

	A	B	C	D	E
1	Ice Cream Sales (boxes)				
2					
3		Vanilla	Chocolate		
4	1992	34	22		
5	1993	38	28		
6	1994	65	44		
7	1995	43	43		
8	1996	89	78		
9	1997	97	102		
10	1998	120	115		**Sales**
11	1999	106	139		**(boxes)**
12					
13					
14					

New data included within border ●

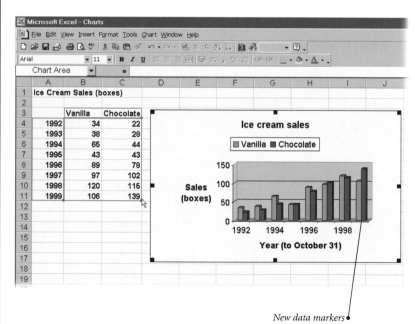

New data markers ●

3 REMOVING SOURCE DATA

● Deleting data from your source worksheet will also cause your chart to update.

● Click on the header for row 4 on your worksheet and drag down to row 5 to select rows 4 and 5.

● Choose **Delete** from the **Edit** menu.

● The 1992 and 1993 sales data are removed, and your chart updates accordingly.

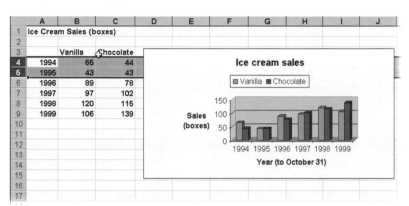

EMBEDDING A CHART IN A NEW LOCATION

If you select a chart and then choose the **Copy** command from the **Edit** menu, the chart is copied to a part of your computer's memory called the Windows clipboard. If you then open another Microsoft Office application, such as Microsoft Word, and choose the **Paste** command, the chart is placed in the new location ⬚. A chart copied to a new location using this method will not update when the source data is updated. If you want automatic updating, select **Paste Special** from the **Edit** menu, click on the **Paste link** radio button in the dialog box, and click on **OK**.

⑩ **Paste**

CHART TYPES

Excel offers a large variety of different chart types – about 11 or so main standard chart types, as well as innumerable sub-types, and various custom types with special features.

LINE CHARTS

A line chart, often called a graph, is perhaps the most familiar type of chart, if only because such charts are commonly used in school math, to plot functions such as $y=x^2-3$. Apart from their use in mathematics, line charts are useful for plotting anything that continually varies and is regularly measured over time or space. A typical use of line charts is to display how a company's stock price changes day by day, as in the example illustrated below.

1 CREATING A LINE CHART

● Rename **Sheet2** in your **Charts.xls** workbook as **Stockprice**. Enter the data shown at right into this worksheet, which shows the weekly stock price of Fantasy Ices measured over several months. Also included is a column listing the level of the fictional Jo Downs Industrial Average over the same period.

	A	B	C	D	E
1	Stock price performance ($)				
2					
3	Date	Fantasy Ices	Jo Downs Average		
4	10-Jul	11	11500		
5	17-Jul	17	11800		
6	24-Jul	15	12080		
7	31-Jul	25	12200		
8	7-Aug	23	11750		
9	14-Aug	39	11900		
10	21-Aug	37	12130		
11	28-Aug	48	12030		
12	4-Sep	52	12070		
13	11-Sep	89	11420		
14					
15					
16					
17					
18					
19					
20					
21					
22					
23					

Sales chart / Salesdata / Chart1 \ Stockprice / Science votes / Scien

● To start, select just the date information and Fantasy Ices stock price data – i.e. the range of cells from A3 to B13. Then click the **Chart Wizard** button on the Standard toolbar.

● In the first dialog box, choose **Line** in the **Chart type:** panel. Accept the default sub-type by clicking on **Next**. Also click on **Next** in the second dialog box.

● In the following dialog box, click on the **Titles** tab if it is not already showing. Name the chart **Stock performance** by keying this in the **Chart title** box. Then type in **Date** to name the **Category (X) axis**, and type **Price ($)** into the **Value (Y) axis** box. Then click on **Next**.

	Date	Fantasy Ices	Jo Downs Average
3	Date	Fantasy Ices	Jo Downs Average
4	10-Jul	11	11500
5	17-Jul	17	11800
6	24-Jul	15	12080
7	31-Jul	25	12200
8	7-Aug	23	11750
9	14-Aug	39	11900
10	21-Aug	37	12130
11	28-Aug	48	12030
12	4-Sep	52	12070
13	11-Sep	89	11420
14			

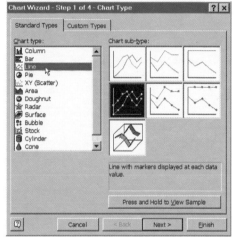

Smooth line…
Excel offers a special option for smoothing out a jagged graph line. To use the option, double-click on the line you want to smooth once you've created the chart. You'll find the Smoothed line option in the **Patterns** section of the dialog box.

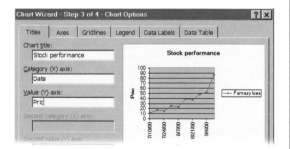

● Click on **Finish** in the
final dialog box to embed
your chart in the
Stockprice worksheet.
Move and resize the chart
if you wish.

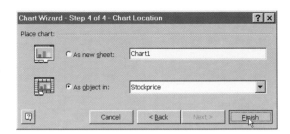

2 ADDING A SECOND LINE

● You now have a chart
showing the performance
of the Fantasy Ices stock
price. But you would like to
add in another line
showing the performance
of the Jo Downs Average,
for comparison.

● Click toward a corner of
your chart to select the
whole chart area. Then
place your mouse pointer
over the blue border at the
corner of cell B13.

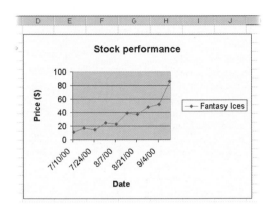

	A	B	C	D	E
1	Stock price performance ($)				
2					
3	Date	Fantasy Ices	Jo Downs Average		S
4	10~Jul	11	11500		
5	17~Jul	17	11800		
6	24~Jul	15	12080		
7	31~Jul	25	12200		
8	7-Aug	23	11750		
9	14-Aug	39	11900		
10	21-Aug	37	12130		
11	28-Aug	48	12030		
12	4-Sep	52	12070		
13	11-Sep	89	11420		
14					
15					

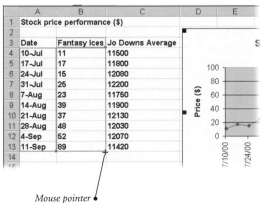

Mouse pointer ●

20 **Moving and Resizing
an Embedded Chart**

● Hold down the mouse button and drag to the right, so that the blue border encompasses cells C3 to C13. This will include the Jo Downs data in your chart. Now release the mouse button.

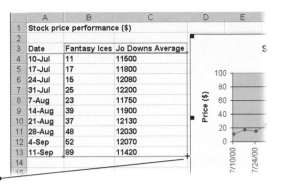

	A	B	C	D	E
1	Stock price performance ($)				
2					
3	Date	Fantasy Ices	Jo Downs Average		
4	10-Jul	11	11500		
5	17-Jul	17	11800		
6	24-Jul	15	12080		
7	31-Jul	25	12200		
8	7-Aug	23	11750		
9	14-Aug	39	11900		
10	21-Aug	37	12130		
11	28-Aug	48	12030		
12	4-Sep	52	12070		
13	11-Sep	89	11420		
14					
15					

Selecting extra data ●

3 A COMBINATION CHART

● Your chart now contains the Jo Downs data, but there is a problem with the chart that stems from the fact that both sets of data have been plotted using the same scale for the value (Y) axis. The two data series are widely spaced and both appear as almost straight lines. What is needed is to plot the two sets of data against different scales. This can be achieved by converting to a combination chart.

● Select the chart area and choose **Chart Type** from the **Chart** menu.

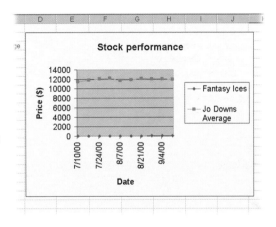

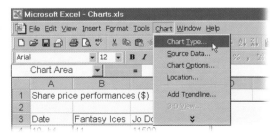

● Click on the **Custom Types** tab.

● Scroll the **Chart type** panel display down by clicking on the arrow at the bottom of the scroll bar, until you see the **Lines on 2 Axes** option.

● Choose the **Lines on 2 Axes** chart type, and then click on **OK**.

● Your chart now appears with the Fantasy Ices stock price plotted against the left-hand vertical axis, and the Jo Downs data plotted against a different scale on the right-hand vertical axis. This is called a combination chart. The chart looks better, but the chart title and axis titles have been lost.

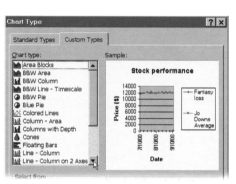

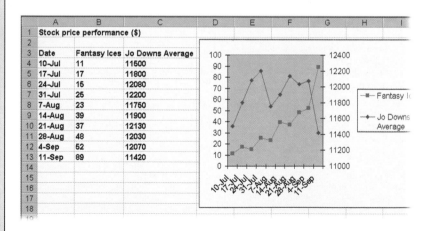

	A	B	C
1	Stock price performance ($)		
2			
3	Date	Fantasy Ices	Jo Downs Average
4	10-Jul	11	11500
5	17-Jul	17	11800
6	24-Jul	15	12080
7	31-Jul	25	12200
8	7-Aug	23	11750
9	14-Aug	39	11900
10	21-Aug	37	12130
11	28-Aug	48	12030
12	4-Sep	52	12070
13	11-Sep	89	11420
14			
15			
16			
17			
18			

4 REINSTATING THE TITLES

● Select the whole chart area, and then choose **Chart Options** from the **Chart** menu.

● This time name the chart **Stock performance vs Jo Downs**, name the **Category (X) axis**, **Date**, and the **Category (Y) axis**, **Price ($)**. Leave the other boxes blank and click on **OK**.

● Your finished combination chart should appear approximately as shown below right.

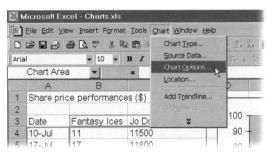

STACKED LINE CHARTS

One of the main sub-types of line chart is a stacked line chart. This is used when there are two or more data series 🗋 and it is desired to show how the data in these series accumulate. For example, the graph line for the second data series is obtained by adding the data for the second data series to the data for the first series. Stacked line charts can be confusing and it is often best to use a column chart or an area chart instead for "stacking" of data.

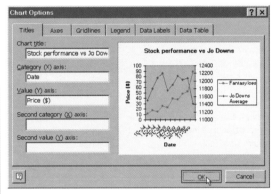

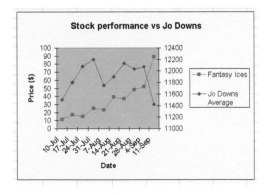

13 ❿ **Data Series**

AREA CHARTS

An area chart is often the most useful type of chart to choose for showing "stacked" or accumulated data. This type of chart enables you to show not just how a particular variable changes over time, but also how the components that make up that variable change over time, and also their changing contributions to the whole. An example would be to chart the increase in a city's population over a century, showing the individual contributions of particular districts of the city to the population increase, as in the example shown below.

1 CREATING AN AREA CHART

● First rename **Sheet3** in your **Charts.xls workbook** as **Population**. Enter the data shown at right into this worksheet. The data shows how a city's population, broken down into its four districts, changed between 1900 and 2000.

● Select any cell in the chart and then click on the **Chart Wizard** button.

Single cell select

If you want to turn a whole block of data-containing cells into a chart, you only need to select one of the cells before clicking the Chart Wizard button.

	A	B	C	D	E	F	G
1	Population of Sun City (thousands)						
2							
3		1900	1925	1950	1975	2000	
4	North district	200	250	500	600	1400	
5	South district	100	300	900	1400	950	
6	West district	310	490	900	1000	850	
7	East district	100	400	1050	1400	1250	
8							
9							

	A	B	C	D	E	F	G
1	Population of Sun City (thousands)						
2							
3		1900	1925	1950	1975	2000	
4	North district	200	250	500	600	1400	
5	South district	100	300	900	1400	950	
6	West district	310	490	900	1000	850	
7	East district	100	400	1050	1400	1250	
8							
9							
10							

Selected cell ●

● Choose **Area** in the **Chart type** panel.
● Choose the middle option in the lower row of sub-types (stacked area with a 3-D visual effect). Click on **Next** and then on **Next** again in the following dialog box.

Chart type choice ●

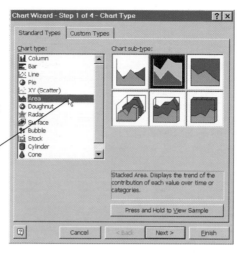

● Stacked area with a 3-D visual effect

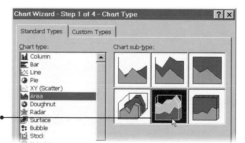

● Give the chart the title **Population of Sun City**, name the **Category (X) axis**, **Year**, and the **Value (Z) axis**, **Population (thousands)**. Click on **Next** and then on **Finish** in the final dialog box. Move and resize your embedded chart if you wish.

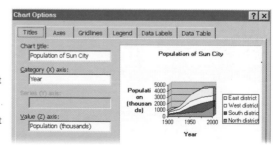

20 **Moving and Resizing an Embedded Chart**

● The chart should look approximately as shown at right. The uppermost line on the chart shows how the total population of Sun City has changed over time. The different colored areas give a sense of how the various districts' contribution to the total has varied over time.

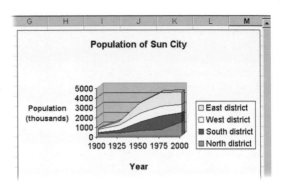

2 CHANGING THE SUB-TYPE

● Rather than charting number totals, you might want to display solely how the components of a variable have changed relative to each other – for example how the percentages of Sun City's population that lived in each district has varied. There is a chart sub-type for doing this as well.

● Select the Chart area and then choose **Chart Type** from the **Chart** menu.

● In the Chart sub-type panel, choose the bottom right option, described as **100% stacked area with a 3-D visual effect**. Click on **OK**.

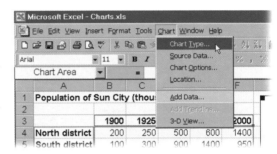

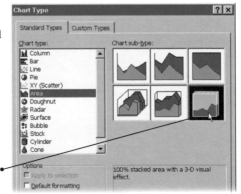

Chosen sub-type ●

• The population chart is now presented purely in terms of the percentage contribution of each district. For example, it can be seen that the percentage contribution of the West district gradually fell over the 20th century, whereas the North district became markedly more popular between 1975 and 2000.

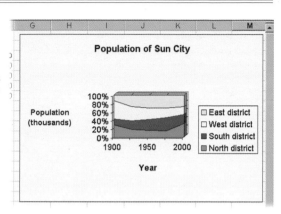

3 DELETING CHART COMPONENTS

• Changing a chart sub-type can sometimes leave you with axis titles that no longer apply or are incorrect. But it's quite easy to edit or remove an axis title. Here we'll remove the vertical axis title.

• Click on the words **Population (thousands)**. A gray box with handles should appear around the words, indicating that they are selected.

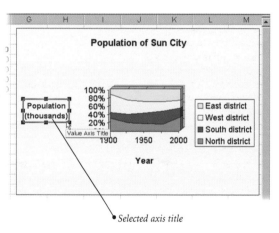

Selected axis title

KEEP IT SIMPLE

In general, you will convey the information in a chart most effectively by keeping the presentation as simple as possible. Try to avoid using too many data series or over-elaborating with the use of colors, fonts, and patterns for titles and backgrounds. Make sure that the chart has a title and that its axes are clearly labeled. However, it is probably better to remove items such as axis titles or legends if they are not strictly necessary.

● Click on the box again using the right mouse button, hold down the mouse button, and choose **Clear** from the shortcut menu.

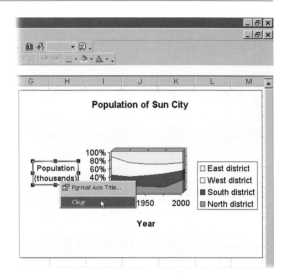

● The axis title is removed, giving more room for the chart itself.

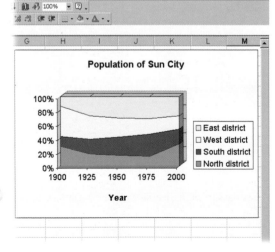

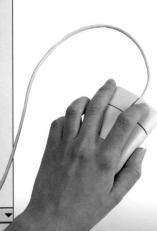

BAR CHARTS

A bar chart is like a column chart tipped onto its side. Instead of displaying data as a series of vertical columns, a bar chart displays it as a series of horizontal bars. Otherwise, there is little difference between the two types of chart. However, because of its shape and layout, a bar chart is often a good choice where the number of categories ⃞ of data is large and the category labels are long.

1 CREATING A BAR CHART

● Choose **Worksheet** from the **Insert** menu to add a new sheet to your **Charts.xls** workbook. Rename this sheet **Scientists**.

● Enter the data shown below right into this worksheet (not worrying if you make some typing mistakes!)

Importing data...
It is often possible to copy tabular data straight into Excel from sources such as World Wide Web pages. This can save a lot of typing. Just drag the mouse to select (highlight) the data you want in the source. Choose **Copy** from the **Edit** menu, open an Excel sheet, and then choose **Paste**.

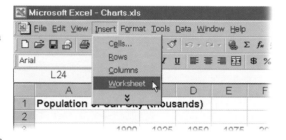

	A	B	C
1	Votes for "Scientist of the Last Millennium"		
2			
3	Galileo Galilei	313	
4	Marie Curie	316	
5	Albert Einstein	412	
6	Isaac Newton	321	
7	Anton van Leeuwenhoek	109	
8	Charles Darwin	418	
9	Lise Meitner	211	
10	Carolus Linnaeus	324	
11	Linus Pauling	215	
12	Dorothy Hodgkin	129	
13	Enrico Fermi	254	
14	Rene Descartes	211	
15	Chandrasekhara Raman	167	
16	Louis Pasteur	256	
17	Nicolaus Copernicus	314	
18			

⓬ **Category Axis**

● Select any cell in the chart and then click on the **Chart Wizard** button.

● Choose **Bar** in the **Chart type** panel and then click on **Next**. Also click on **Next** in the second dialog box.

● Give the chart the title **Votes for Scientist of the Last Millennium**. Click on **Next**.

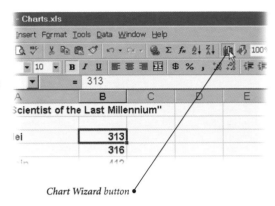

Chart Wizard button ●

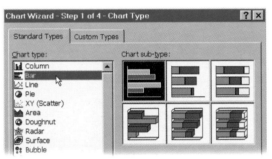

CUSTOM TYPES

As well as the standard chart types and sub-types, you'll find various unusual chart presentations, most with ready-made formatting, in the **Custom Types** section (just click on the **Custom Types** tab in the first **Chart Wizard** dialog box). Bar chart variants, for example, include a rustic-looking one named **Outdoor Bars**, and something more avant-garde called **Tubes**.

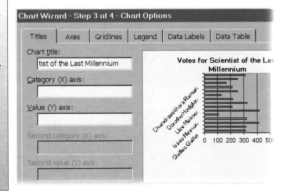

● Choose to display the chart **as a new sheet**, named **Science votes**. Then click on **Finish**.

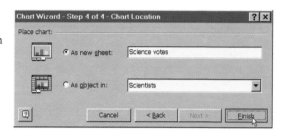

● This bar chart clearly displays the voting for each scientist, and there is plenty of room for the names of the scientists. Because there is only one data series in this instance, the legend is unnecessary and you might wish to remove it.

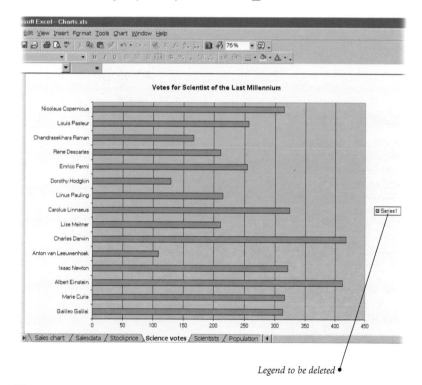

Legend to be deleted ●

 ⑩ Data Series

13

PIE CHARTS

If you want to present some data that shows how an entity (e.g., sales of a product) divides up into component parts (e.g., sales of that product by region), you should use a pie chart. A pie chart shows how the whole item (the "pie") splits up into its components (the "slices"). A pie chart has a single data series 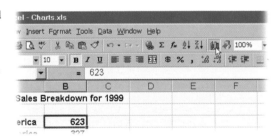 and, unlike most charts, has no chart axes. Try the exercises to see how pie charts work.

1 CREATING A PIE CHART

● Insert a new worksheet in your **Charts.xls** workbook and call it **Regional Sales**. Then enter the data shown at right in the worksheet.

● Select any cell in the data table and then click on the **Chart Wizard** button.

● In the first **Chart Wizard** dialog box, choose **Pie** under **Chart type**. Accept the default chart type shown by clicking on **Next**. Also click on **Next** in the second **Chart Wizard** dialog box.

	A	B	C	D	E
1	Regional Sales Breakdown for 1999				
2					
3	North America	623			
4	South America	327			
5	Europe	389			
6	Asia	123			
7	Africa	432			
8	Australia	178			
9					

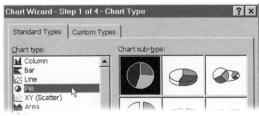

❿ **Data Series**

● It's always a good idea to give a chart a title. Click in the **Chart title** box and type **Breakdown of 1999 Sales by Region**. Then click on the **Data Labels** tab.

● You have some choices for labeling the slices of the pie. It can be helpful to show what percentage each slice of the pie represents. So choose the **Show percent** option. Then click on **Next**.

● In the final dialog box, choose **As new sheet**, name the chart **Regional sales chart**, and then click on **Finish**.

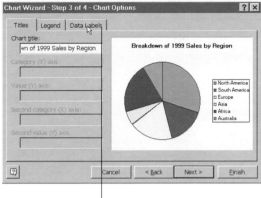

Data labels tab ●

Show percent option ●

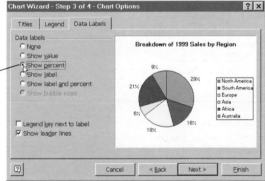

COMBINING LABELS

You can often improve the clarity of a pie chart by dispensing with the legend and instead fully labeling each slice of the pie. To do this, choose the **Show label and percent** option in the **Data Labels** section of the third **Chart Wizard** dialog box. Then switch to the **Legend** section and cancel the **Show legend** box.

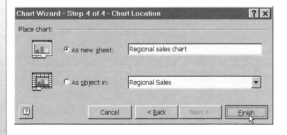

● You now have a pie chart that shows the breakdown of 1999 sales by region. The Excel program has automatically calculated the percentage of sales that have been made in each region, and has labeled the "slices" accordingly.

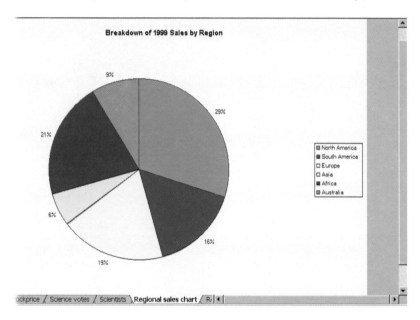

2 A 3-D EXPLODED CHART

● For a more graphic approach, you might want to change your 2-D chart to a 3-D one, and separate the pie "slices" a little. This is called an "exploded" pie chart.

● Choose **Chart Type** from the **Chart** menu.

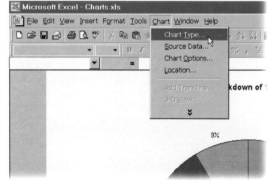

● In the **Chart sub-type** panel, choose the middle option in the lower row, and then click on **OK**.

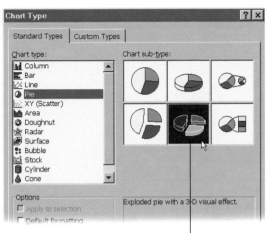

Exploded pie option ●

● The sales data are now graphically represented in an exploded pie chart. By showing the sales of each region as a separate three dimensional object, with depth as well as area, it is easier to compare the regions' sales visually.

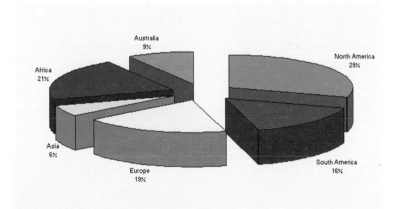

FORMATTING A CHART

Once you have created a chart, you will often want to format it to improve its appearance. You can format any part of a chart but in this chapter you'll practice formatting the chart axes.

FORMATTING THE AXES

The chart that you are going to format is the **Stockprice** line chart that you created on pages 28–33. You should find it in the **Stockprice** sheet of your **Charts.xls** workbook. If you have not already created

the chart you should do so now. The first chart components that you'll format are the chart's axes, of which there are three – a horizontal Category axis (X-axis) and two vertical Value axes (Y-axes).

1 PREPARING TO FORMAT

● First click on the chart area of your embedded chart, choose **Location** from the **Chart** menu, choose **As new sheet** in the dialog box, and rename the chart **Price Chart**.

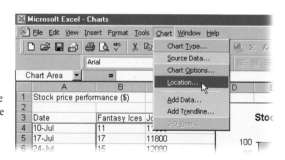

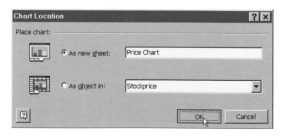

 ⑫ Category Axis

 ❹ Value Axis

2 FORMATTING THE CATEGORY AXIS

● Double-click on the **Category Axis** (X-axis). This brings up the **Format** **Axis** dialog box. For the purpose of this example, we are going to suppose that you would like to color the axis, make it a little thicker, and simplify the axis labeling to just months, with no tick marks (little lines) dividing up the axis.

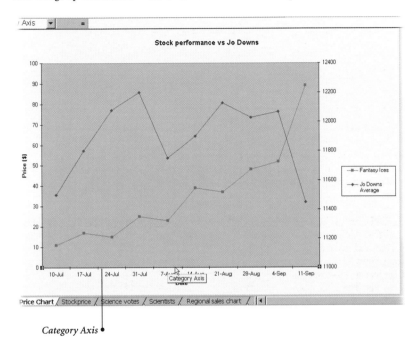

Category Axis ●

FORMATTING PRINCIPLES

Each of the chart components – the axes, titles, data series, legend, and background areas – can be formatted separately. Although only axis formatting is covered in this section, the same methods apply to formatting other components. The main ways to format components are by color, font, and type size (for text), alignment, style, and weight (for lines), pattern and border (for background areas), and number format (for axis labels). You may need to experiment to obtain a satisfactory result.

● Click the down arrow next to **Automatic** in the Color box of the **Patterns** section. Choose a color – say, orange.

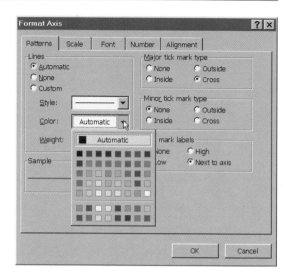

● Now click the down arrow at the right of the **Weight** box and choose a heavier weight (thickness) for the line.
● Under **Major tick mark type**, click the **None** option. Then click the **Number** tab.

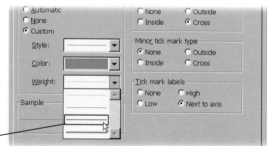

Choosing a heavier weight ●

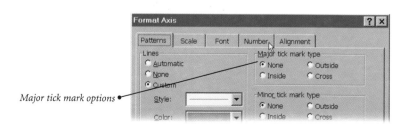

Major tick mark options ●

● In the **Number** section, under **Type**, scroll down and choose an option that will display only months for the dates on the X-axis (for example, Mar-98).

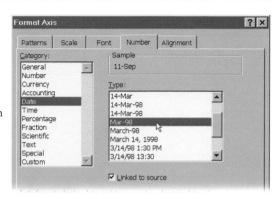

● Now go to the **Font** section. You use this section to define the font of the labeling – which includes the typeface, type size, and color of the labels. Choose a TrueType (TT) font (for example, Garamond). Choose **Bold** under **Font style**, 16 pt under **Size**, and the same color as you gave the axis line (e.g., orange). Then click **OK**.

● The axis should now appear as shown below right.

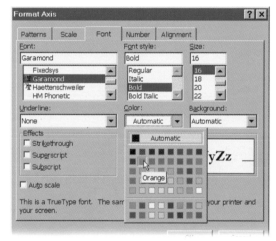

TrueType Fonts...
TrueType fonts are fonts that look exactly the same on screen as they do when printed. They can be printed on any type of printer. Sticking to TrueType fonts makes documents more portable because they will look the same when printed on different printers.

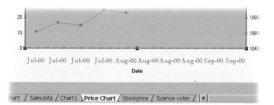

● Double-click the Category axis, and close the **Scale** tab in the **Format Axis** dialog box. Now change the number in the box labeled **Number of categories between tick-mark labels** from 1 to 4. This will reduce the number of labels that appear underneath the axis. Now click **OK**.

● The Category axis should appear as shown below.

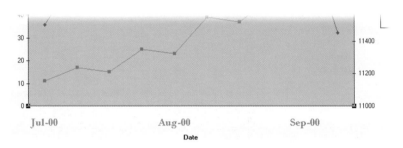

3 FORMATTING THE FIRST VALUE AXIS

● Double-click on the first (left-hand) **Value axis** to open the **Format Axis** dialog box. Let's suppose you want to give this axis a different font, color both the axis line and labels green, and put $ signs on the labels.

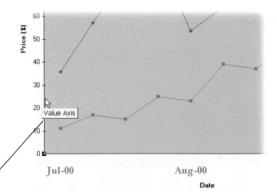

Value Axis ●

● In the **Patterns** section, choose a light, bright, green line for the axis. Then click the **Font** tab.

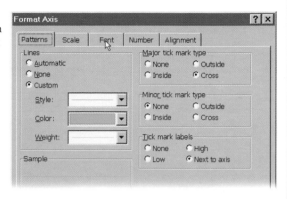

● In the **Font** section, choose **Arial** (or another TrueType font), **Bold**, **11 pt**, and the same bright green for the labels. Now click the **Number** tab.

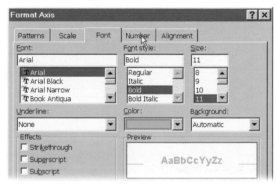

● In the **Number** section, choose **Currency** under **Category**. This is because you want to give the labels a currency format, adding dollar signs. Now click **OK**.

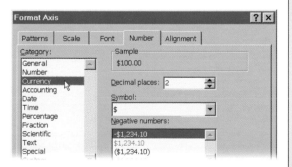

● The chart should now appear as shown below. However, you may have noticed that the chart is a bit misleading because the left-hand axis stock price runs from $0.00 up to $100.00, while the right-hand axis (used to plot the Jo Downs Average) runs only from 11,000 to 12,400. To give a more informative comparison, the right-hand axis should also start at 0. So you'll fix that next.

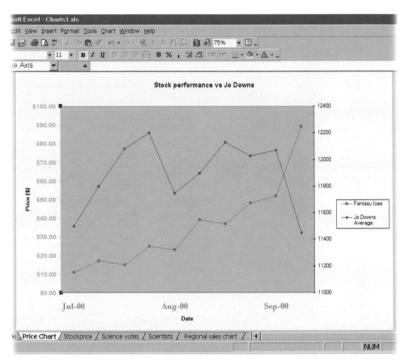

LINEAR OR LOGARITHMIC?

The standard axis scale is a linear one, for example, $10, $20, $30, $40, and so on. A logarithmic scale, in contrast, has check marks that are each a constant multiple of the previous one, for example 1, 10, 100, 1000, and so on. Logarithmic scales are useful for plotting variables that exhibit very rapid change. To switch from linear to logarithmic, check the **Logarithmic scale** box in the **Scale** section of the **Format Axis** dialog box.

4 THE SECOND VALUE AXIS

● Double-click on the right-hand Secondary Value axis.

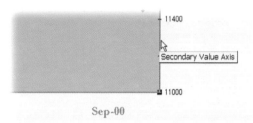

Sep-00

● In the **Scale** section, enter the number 0 in the **Minimum** box. This will set the scale to run from 0. Turn off the **Minor unit** box, check the **Major unit** box, and change its value from 200 to 2000.

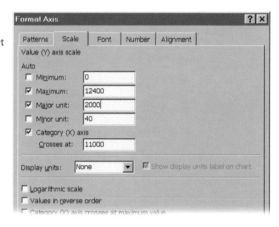

● In the **Patterns** section, choose a bright color different from the color you used for the first value axis (red for instance), and increase the weight of the axis line.

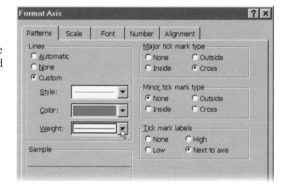

● In the **Font** section, choose a different TrueType font, make it **Bold** and **12 pt**, and select the same color that you used for the axis line.

● Finally, in the **Number** section, choose **Number** under **Category** and check the **Use 1000 Separator** box. This will put a comma in the large numbers used as labels for this axis. Finally, click **OK**.

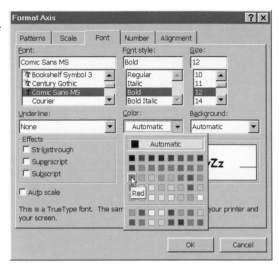

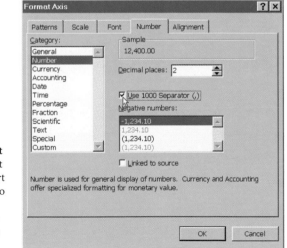

Shortcut to the dialog box...

To bring up the **Format** dialog box, you can just double-click on the part of the chart you want to format. If you have problems with double-clicking, just click once on the part, and then press the [Ctrl] key and 1 at the same time.

● The chart should now appear as shown below. It now gives a much more accurate picture of the plotted items – compared with the soaring Fantasy Ices stock price, the Jo Downs performance has been flat for months. Save your **Charts.xls** workbook by clicking the **Save** button on the Standard toolbar.

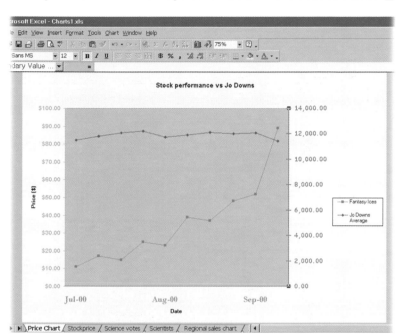

COORDINATING DATA SERIES AND AXES

If you use a combination line chart to plot different data series against different scales on the two axes, it's a good idea to add a visual device to indicate which axis goes with which data series.

For example, you may choose to color each axis the same as its corresponding data series. Anything that will aid the understanding of the chart is well worth implementing.

❸ Save Workbook

EXCEL GRAPHICS

As well as its charting features, the Excel program also offers a
selection of tools to embellish your charts and worksheets. To
create graphics, you use a special Drawing toolbar.

CREATING AND FORMATTING SHAPES

The following exercise will familiarize you
with some of the basic tools for creating
graphics in Excel. You'll create a simple
logo for the ice-cream business, Fantasy
Ices. The logo consists of a picture of a
cone wafer containing a scoop of
strawberry ice cream, together with the
words "Fantasy Ices." You'll create and
format the separate elements of the logo,
then you'll combine them together. First
insert a new worksheet in your **Charts.xls**
workbook and call it **logo**.

1 THE DRAWING TOOLBAR

● Click the **Drawing**
button on the Standard
toolbar. The Drawing
toolbar will appear below
the worksheet.

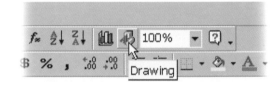

2 DRAWING BASIC SHAPES

● Click the **AutoShapes**
button on the Drawing
toolbar.

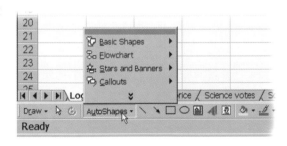

● Choose **Basic Shapes** from the menu. An array of basic shapes should appear to the right. Choose **Isosceles Triangle**.

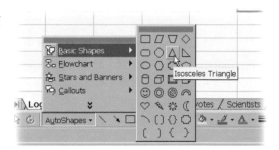

● Now click the center of cell B4, hold down the mouse button and drag the mouse pointer down and across to the left-hand edge of cell B15. You should see an isosceles triangle. Now release the mouse button.

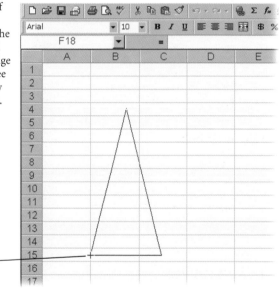

Mouse pointer ●

● Click the **Oval** button on the Drawing toolbar. You use this button to draw either ellipses or circles.

● Hold down the ⟨⇧ Shift⟩ key (this tells Excel that you want to draw a circle). Click the left top corner of cell E7. Hold down the mouse button and drag the mouse pointer down and to the right to cell F11. This creates a circle with a diameter slightly smaller than the base of the triangle. Now release both the mouse button and the ⟨⇧ Shift⟩ key.

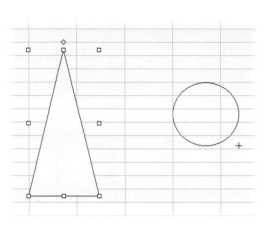

3 ROTATING THE TRIANGLE

● Click the triangle to select it. Now click the **Free Rotate** button on the Drawing toolbar.

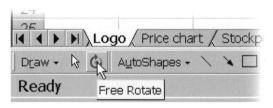

● Place the mouse pointer, which is now a rotate symbol, over the bottom left corner of the triangle. Press down on the mouse button.

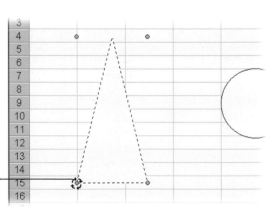

Mouse pointer •

● Now drag the mouse pointer up and to the right until you reach the position shown at right. Release the mouse button.

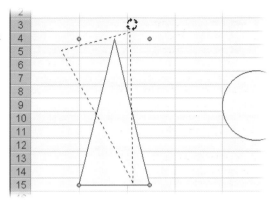

4 COLORING IN THE TRIANGLE

● Click the down arrow next to the **Fill Color** button (a tipping paint pot) on the Drawing toolbar. Click the **Fill Effects** button.

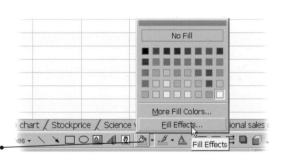

Fill Color button ●

● Choose the **Pattern** tab in the **Fill Effects** dialog box.

Pattern tab ●

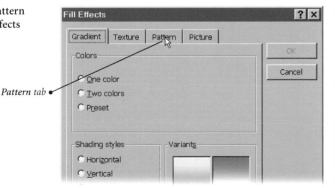

● Click the down-arrow next to the **Foreground** box and choose **Gold** from the color palette.

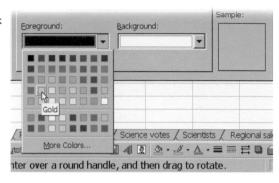

● Now click the down-arrow next to the **Background** box and choose **Light Orange** for your cone's background color.

● Choose whatever you like in the main **Pattern** array to pattern the "cone," and then click **OK**.

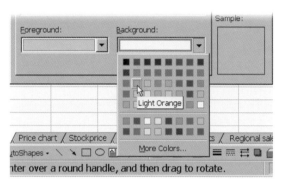

Textures…

You can give a surface texture to any shape you create by using the **Texture** section in the **Fill Effects** dialog box. Available textures include various stone, marble, wood, fabric, matting, crumpled paper, and water-on-glass effects.

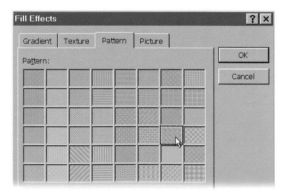

● Your "ice-cream cone" should now appear in a colored form as shown below. Next, click on the down-arrow next to the **Line Color** button, which is to be found on the Drawing toolbar, and choose **No Line**. This removes the black border that currently runs around the object.

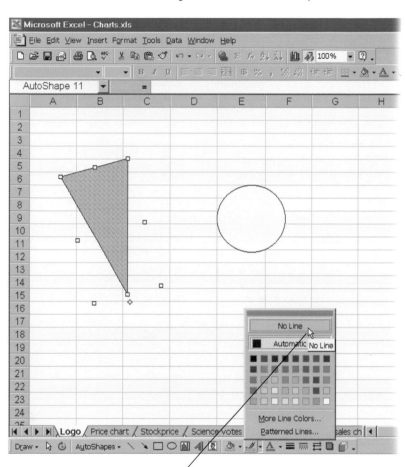

*Selecting **No Line** removes the black border* ●

5 COLORING THE CIRCLE

● Click the Circle to select it. Click the down arrow next to the **Fill Color** button and choose **Fill Effects**.

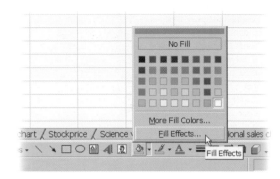

● In the **Gradient** section of the **Fill Effects** dialog box, under **Colors**, choose **Two colors**.

● Click the down-arrow next to the **Color 1** box, and then click on the **More Colors** button.

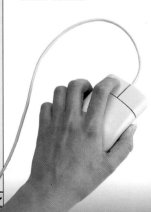

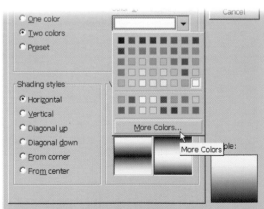

● In the **Colors** dialog box, choose a light pink and then click **OK**.

● Repeat the last two steps for the **Color 2** box, but this time choose a much deeper pink.

● Under **Shading styles** choose **Diagonal down**, and then click **OK**.

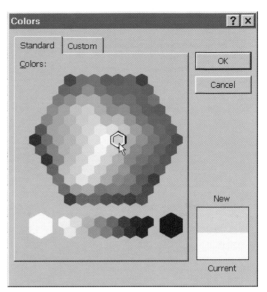

COLOR PICKING

The color picker hexagon in the **Colors** dialog box provides a total of 127 different colors, plus black, white, and 17 shades of gray. For a more extensive choice, choose the **Custom** section of the **Colors** dialog box. This offers you the amazing choice of over 16 million different colors.

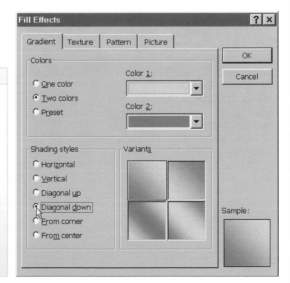

● The "scoop of ice cream" should now look as shown at right. Now click on the little down-arrow next to the **Line Color** button and choose **No Line**.

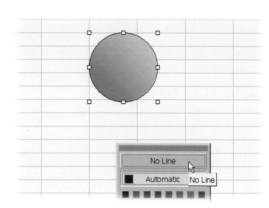

6 COMBINING THE SHAPES

● Click the pink ice cream, and holding down the mouse button, drag it up and to the left until it sits over the mouth of the "cone." Then release.

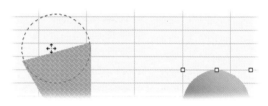

● Your graphic should appear as shown at right. You now want to place the cone on top of the ice-cream graphic so that it looks like the ice cream is sitting inside the cone. So you need to define for Excel which graphic should cover the other in the area they overlap.

Combine the two shapes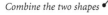

● With the pink ice cream selected, click the small arrow to the right of the **Draw** button on the Drawing toolbar.

● Choose **Order** in the menu, and **Send to Back** in the submenu. This will put the ice cream behind the cone.

● The frozen treat should now appear as shown below.

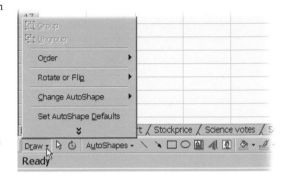

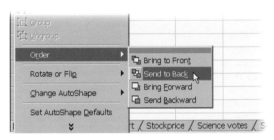

Grouping objects…

Once you've combined a number of separate objects, you should consider grouping them. Grouped objects behave as if they were one object, which is useful for purposes such as moving, resizing, or copying. To group objects, first select them by holding down the ⟨ Shift ⟩ key and clicking on each object in turn. Then click the **Draw** button on the Drawing toolbar and choose **Group** from the pop-up menu.

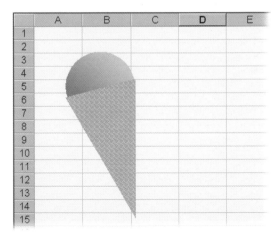

ADDING DECORATIVE TEXT

One of the easiest ways to incorporate some text into a graphic logo is to use the WordArt feature. This provides a variety of different template ideas for text graphics, which you can modify as much as you like in terms of font, type size, alignment, and so on. There's even a special WordArt toolbar that allows you to curve text in various directions or modify the text kerning (spacing between letters).

1 PICKING A WORDART STYLE

● Click on a cell to the right of your ice cream. Then click the **Insert WordArt** button on the Drawing toolbar.

● In the **WordArt Gallery**, choose the third option from the right in the bottom row, and then click **OK**.

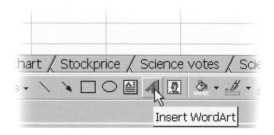

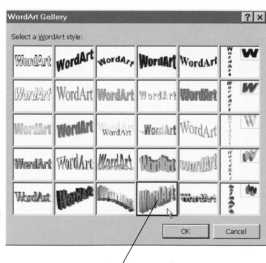

WordArt option ●

2 TYPING THE TEXT

● In the **Edit WordArt Text** dialog box, just type your text – in this case, **Fantasy Ices**. Then click OK.

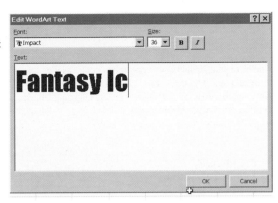

3 THE WORDART TOOLBAR

● The WordArt object appears on the sheet. The WordArt toolbar is also displayed. This can be used to perform various operations, such as rotating or realigning the WordArt. But you don't need to do so at the moment, so click on the toolbar's **Close** button.

The WordArt toolbar

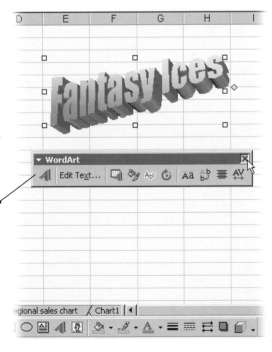

4 FORMATTING THE WORDART

● You can format WordArt in the same way as any drawn object. With the WordArt selected, click the down-arrow next to the **Fill Color** button. Choose **Fill Effects**.

Fill color button ●

● Choose a gradient of colors for your WordArt in the same way as you did for your ice cream. Using the same colors as for the ice cream could be a good idea, but this time try a different Shading style, such as the **From center** option. Then click **OK**.

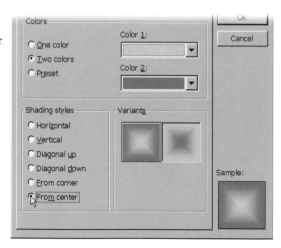

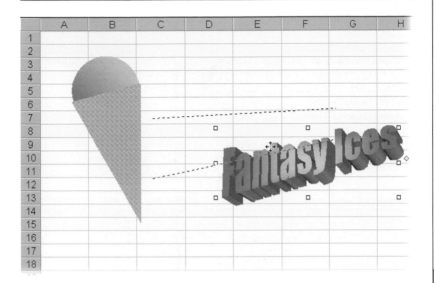

● Click on the WordArt and, holding down the mouse button, drag to move it a little closer to the ice-cream cone.

● When you are satisfied with the position of the WordArt object in relation to the ice-cream cone, release the mouse button.

● Click off the WordArt object to remove the handles, and to see the final effect on the sheet.

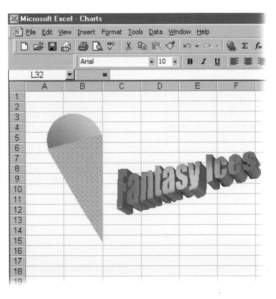

GLOSSARY

AXIS
A straight line used as a reference for plotting data on a chart. Most charts have two axes – a horizontal one, the X-axis, and a vertical one, the Y-axis. A 3-D chart has three axes, termed the X, Y, and Z axes, which are all perpendicular to each other.

AXIS TITLE
Text that describes what is plotted along a particular axis.

CATEGORIES
Individual measurement intervals or groupings for charted data. In most charts, these are the labels that you can see along the horizontal axis.

CATEGORY AXIS
A line along which labels for a chart's categories are arranged. In most charts (except for bar charts), this is the horizontal line (X-axis) along the bottom of the chart. In bar charts, it is the vertical axis.

CHART AREA
The whole area enclosing a chart, includes the axis titles, chart titles, and legend. When a chart is moved or resized, this involves the whole chart area.

CHART WIZARD
A subprogram that guides you through the basic process of creating a chart. The Chart Wizard gives little guidance on formatting, however.

COMBINATION CHART
A chart that uses different value axes for plotting different data series against.

DATA MARKER
A piece of data plotted on a chart. It corresponds to the data in a single worksheet cell. It might be a single column, a cross or square, or a pie "slice," depending on the type of chart.

DATA SERIES
A collection of data markers, usually corresponding to the data within a column or row of cells in a worksheet. A data series might be seen as a series of columns, or as squares or crosses joined by a line.

GRAPH
A chart in which the data markers in a series are joined by a line – i.e. a line chart.

GROUPED OBJECT
A number of drawn objects that have been grouped together as one, using the Group command.

GRIDLINES
Guidelines, horizontal or vertical, that appear behind charted data and assist you to read off the value of a data marker by reference to a scale.

HANDLES
Small black boxes that appear around the perimeter of a drawn object or part of a chart after it has been selected. The black boxes indicate that you can move, resize, format, or remove the object.

LEGEND
A key that explains the data series in a chart.

NUMERICAL VALUE
A number, date, time, percentage, or monetary amount.

PLOT AREA
A rectangular region of a chart that includes the charted data. In 3D charts, the plot area may also enclose the chart axes and the axis titles.

RANGE
A block of cells.

SCALE
A collection of properties pertaining to the axis of a chart that include the number and arrangement of category or value labels that are spaced along the axis, and the minimum and maximum values that are plottable (for value axes).

SOURCE DATA
Data in a worksheet that have been used to create a chart.

TICK MARK
A marker that divides two categories on the category axis of a chart.

VALUE AXIS
A line along which the measurement units for some plotted data are arranged. The magnitude of each piece of data (its value) is plotted against this axis. In most charts (except bar charts), the value axis is the vertical, or Y, axis.

WALLS AND FLOOR
In 3D charts, the boundaries of the region defined by the chart's axes. The walls and floor can be formatted separately from the remainder of the plot area.

INDEX

ACKNOWLEDGMENTS

PUBLISHER'S ACKNOWLEDGMENTS

Dorling Kindersley would like to thank the following:
Paul Mattock of APM, Brighton, for commissioned photography.
Microsoft Corporation for permission to reproduce screens
from within Microsoft® Excel.

*Every effort has been made to trace the copyright holders.
The publisher apologizes for any unintentional omissions and would be pleased,
in such cases, to place an acknowledgment in future editions of this book.*

Microsoft is a registered trademark of Microsoft Corporation
in the United States and/or other countries.